CARBOHYDRATES!
FOODS THAT GIVE POSITIVE ENERGY!
HEALTHY EATING FOR KIDS
CHILDREN'S DIET & NUTRITION BOOKS

All Rights reserved. No part of this book may be reproduced or used in any way or form or by any means whether electronic or mechanical, this means that you cannot record or photocopy any material ideas or tips that are provided in this book

Copyright 2016

A big source of energy for the body is carbohydrates. We can obtain them from plants and dairy products. The three kinds of carbohydrates are starch, sugar and fiber.

Healthy high fiber carbohydrates should be taken in moderation. They will help you maintain your body's healthy weight. If you consume too much of them, there is a risk that you will gain weight. Too much carbohydrates can also lead to high blood pressure, especially for those who have diabetes.

Our carbohydrate intake should be kept balanced. We need 40% to 60% of calories from carbohydrates every day. If it is lower than this, it is considered unhealthy. For adults, the recommended daily allowance for carbohydrates is 130 grams.

QUINOA

This nutritious seed has become popular in the natural health community. This nutritious seed is prepared and eaten like a grain. Cooked quinoa can provide you 21.3% carbohydrates. It is a high-carb food. Moreover, it is also a good source of fiber and protein.

OATS

Oats are a great source of many antioxidants, vitamins and minerals. About 66% carbohydrates are present in raw oats. Eating oats can give us health benefits like lower blood sugar levels, especially for people with diabetes. Oats can lower your cholesterol levels and may reduce the risk of heart disease.

BUCKWHEAT

It is also classified as a pseudocereal. Raw buckwheat can supply 71.5% carbohydrates. On the other hand, cooked buckwheat groats can supply 20% carbohydrates. This nutritious food also contain protein and fiber. Buckwheat has more antioxidants and minerals than most grains.

BANANAS

They are among the most popular fruits in the world. These fruits can provide 23% carbohydrates, in the form of starch or sugar. Bananas that are not ripe contain more starches. As the banana ripens, these starches transform into natural sugars. These popular fruits also contain Vitamin B6, Vitamin C and potassium.

SWEET POTATOES

These are a delicious and nutritious tuber. If sweet potatoes are cooked, they can supply 18-21% carbohydrates. These carbohydrates contain starch, fiber and sugar.

BEETROOTS

These root vegetables come in a purple color. They are most commonly called beets. Beets contain 8-10% of carbohydrates either raw or cooked. Aside from that, beets also contain vitamins, minerals, antioxidants and plant compounds. Beets can improve health and boost physical performance.

ORANGES

These fruits are very popular all around the world. Oranges are mainly composed of water. They can provide 11.8% carbohydrates. These amazing fruits are also a good source of fiber. Consuming oranges may help prevent kidney stones and may improve heart health. They can also prevent anemia.

BLUEBERRIES

These are very delicious fruits. Because of their powerful plant compounds and antioxidants, they are often called a superfood. Blueberries contain mostly water. They also contain 14.5% carbohydrates.

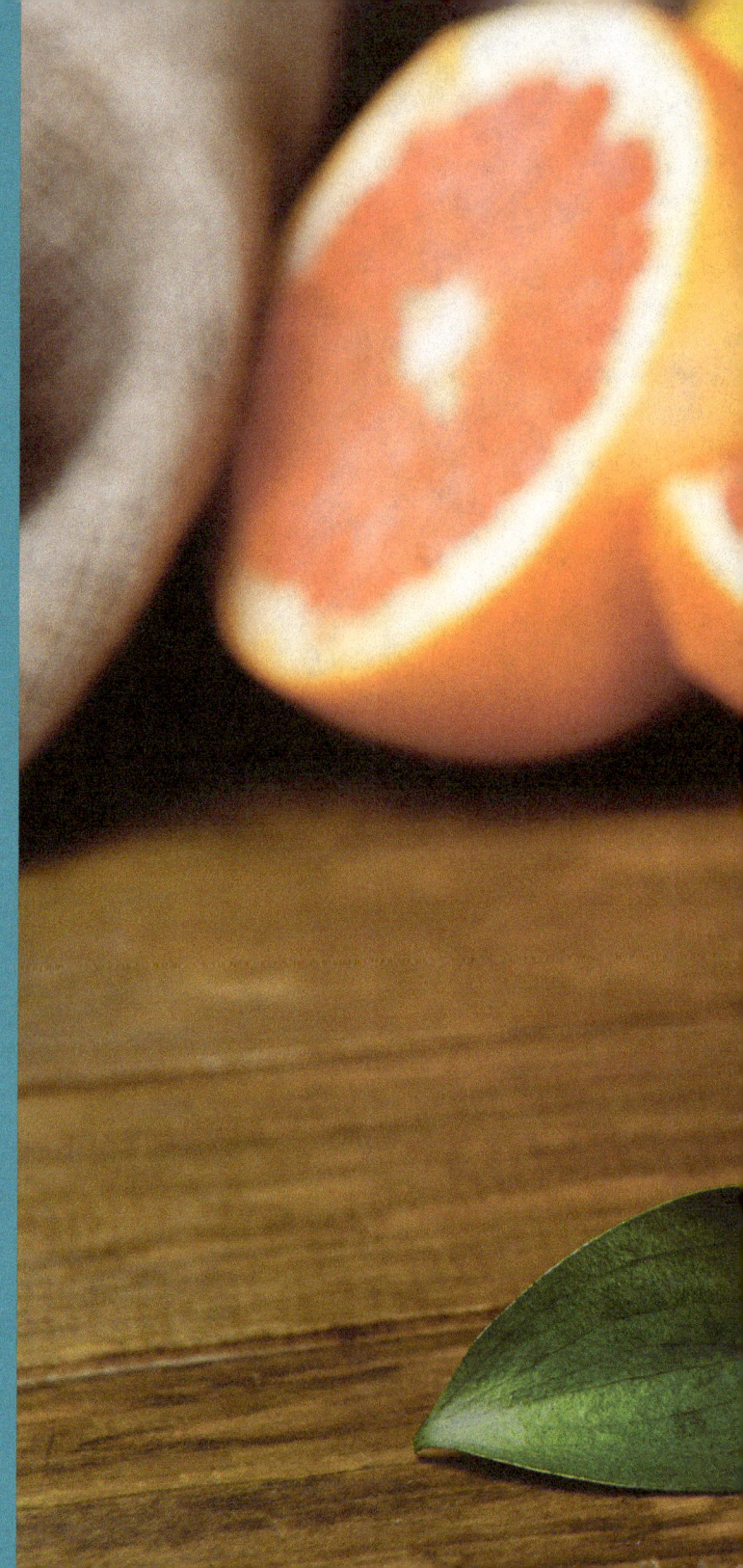

GRAPEFRUIT

These citrus fruits taste sweet, bitter and sour. Grapefruit can provide the body with high amounts of vitamins and minerals. These fruits can aid weight loss and reduce insulin resistance.

APPLES

These fruits taste sweet and have a distinctive crunch. They contain 13-15% carbohydrates. Apples are a good source of Vitamin C, antioxidants and healthy plant compounds. Apples may help improve blood sugar control, reduce the risk of heart disease and decrease the risk of some types of cancer.

KIDNEY BEANS

These belong to the legume family. They can give you 22.8% carbohydrates. These carbohydrates are in the form of starches and fiber. Kidney beans are also high in protein. These beans contain high amounts of antioxidants. These include anthocyanins and isoflavones.

CHICKPEAS

They are commonly known as garbanzo beans. They are also part of the legume family. Cooked chickpeas can provide the body with 27.4% carbohydrates, about 8% of which is fiber. Chickpeas are also a good source of protein.

BREAD

Eating bread can give us nutrients. We need these nutrients for the growth and maintenance of our health and the well being of our body. Bread is a good source of fiber, vitamins, minerals and carbohydrates. Whole grain bread can give us 20 grams of carbohydrates.

PASTA

White and semolina pasta are good sources of carbohydrates and glycemic acid. Consuming three cups of spaghetti pasta can give us 97% of carbohydrates.

GREEN VEGETABLES

Numerous green vegetables are good sources of carbohydrates. These vegetables are also packed with important minerals and vitamins. These veggies are high in nutrients.

The right amount of carbohydrates in the body can give us steady energy. They keep blood sugar levels steady. The world's healthiest foods are rich in carbohydrates. Why not have these foods on your table and be amazed at how good eating them makes you feel?

www.ingramcontent.com/pod-product-compliance
Lightning Source LLC
LaVergne TN
LVHW061321060426
835507LV00019B/2255